WEST VIRGINIA IN
PICTURES

Edited by Steve Payne

Quarrier Press
Charleston, West Virginia

10 9 8 7 6 5 4 3 2 • Printed in China

Library of Congress Catalog Card Number: 00-102057
ISBN: 1-891852-09-4

Distributed by:
Pictorial Histories Distribution • 1416 Quarrier St. • Charleston, WV 25301

phd@intelos.net

PHOTOGRAPHY BY STEVE PAYNE   www.stevepayne.com

(except as listed below:)

STEPHEN J. SHALUTA, JR.
Cranberry Glades (2), Wheeling Suspension Bridge, Bowers Homestead,
Harpers Ferry, John Henry Monument, Cardinals, Glass Blower,
Italian Heritage Festival, Tygart Lake State Park, Black Bear, Groundhog,
Beckley Exhibition Mine, Canaan Valley State Park

DAVID FATTALEH
Hawks Nest, Tamarack, Barn Owl, Harpers Ferry Architecture, Bridge Day

LARRY BELCHER
Rhododendren, Mail Pouch Barn

West Virginia Hills (state song of West Virginia)

Oh, the West Virginia hills!
How majestic and how grand,
With their summits bathed in glory,
Like our Prince Immanuel's Land!
Is it any wonder then,
That my heart with rapture thrills,
As I stand once more with loved ones
On those West Virginia Hills.

Chorus:
Oh, the hills, beautiful hills
How I love those West Virginia hills!
If o'er sea or land I roam,
Still I'll think of happy home,
And the friends among the West Virginia hills.

◄ ◄ *Blackwater Falls State Park in winter*
◄ *Cranberry Glades*
Rock Climbing ►
Wheeling Suspension Bridge ► ►

◄ *John Henry Monument near Talcott*
Rhododendron, state flower (Rhododendron maximum)
Pricketts Fort State Park ▶ ▶
Male and female cardinals, state bird ▶ ▶ ▶

◀ *Ritter Park, Huntington*
  Pink dogwood ▶

Glass blower, Wellsburg ◀
Covered bridge at Philippi, site of first land battle,
U.S. Civil War ▶
Italian Heritage Festival, Clarksburg ▶ ▶
Tygart Lake State Park ▶ ▶ ▶

◄ *Barn owl*
West Virginia University "Mountaineer" football ►
Coopers Rock State Forest ► ►
Black bear, state animal ► ► ►

◄ *Groundhog*
Wildflowers ►
Holly River State Park ► ►
Architecture of Harpers Ferry ►

◀ *Shay Locomotive at Cass Scenic Railroad State*
Babcock State Park ▶
Fall harvest at Marlinton ▶ ▶
Snowshoe Mountain Resort ▶ ▶ ▶

◄ *Regatta fireworks, Charleston*
Bruceton Mills ▶
Whitetail deer ▶ ▶
Pocahontas County farm ▶ ▶ ▶

◀ *Hills Creek Falls*
Marshall University "Thundering Herd" football ▶

◄ *Dolly Sods*
The Greenbrier at White Sulphur Springs

◀ *Almost heaven*
Sternwheeling on the Kanawha River ▶

◀ *Black-eyed susans*
Bridge Day at Fayetteville ▶
Old barn near Snowshoe ▶ ▶
Droop Mountain State Park battle re-enactors ▶ ▶ ▶

State Flower — Rhododendron
State Bird — Cardinal
State Butterfly — Monarch Butterfly
State Fruit — Golden Delicious Apple
State Fish — Brook Trout
State Animal — Black Bear
State Tree — Sugar Maple
West Virginia Day — June 20th
State Songs — West Virginia Hills
          This Is My West Virginia
          West Virginia My Home Sweet Home
Area — 24,231.4 square miles
Population — 1,793,477
Counties — 55
High Elevation — Spruce Knob, 4861 feet
Low Elevation — Harpers Ferry, 247 feet
Geographic center of the State — near Sutton

◄ *Sunset in the mountains*